Sent From Heaven!

Why You Are Here

by

Carolyn Priester Jones

Mountjoy
Press

Sent From Heaven – Why You Are Here...

ISBN:
979-8-9914842-2-0 Print Edition
979-8-9914842-3-7 E-Pub via Kindle

CONTENTS

DEDICATION

I dedicate this Life and this book to The Creator of the Joy and Music in my life — my Father God.

I praise God and thank Him for walking with me and talking with me. I thank Him for giving me the Words of this book. I thank Him for all the other lessons He has taught me. I thank Him for allowing me to be His "why" child and ask Him unending questions. I thank Him for forgiving me and allowing too many "do overs" to count. I love our life together. I look forward to an Eternity of sharing our Love!

Carolyn Priester Jones
March 25, 2025

ACKNOWLEDGEMENTS

I thank God for putting me in a family who made it easy to understand God's Love and Grace.

I thank God for His Pure Love revealed in all the seasons He gave my parents, Horace and Pearl Priester.

I thank God for giving me a true soulmate in Jay Jones, my husband of 47 years. Using his gift of added dimension, Jay constantly shows me the wonders of God's World. His creativity and ingenuity continue to amaze me.

Jay and I have been partners in teaching, video production and writing books. This book, as well as numerous other projects, would not have come to life without Jay.

Someone once said of us, "She dreams it up, but he makes it happen."

I am blessed to be married to Jay, who makes my dreams come true!

Foreward

God gave us many wonderful Truths through The Bible.

However, He did not give us everything in Words. Sometimes His Words are an invitation to come closer to Him and let Him whisper a secret or two right into our ears.

He talks directly to us. We may hear him audibly, like we hear human voices, but more often He will speak into our spirits. He will put thoughts in our minds. He will cause us to wonder about things.

He welcomes our questions. He answers them in His Way and His Time. And the answers are not always what we thought they would be.

He delights in surprising us!

This book has been His Surprise Package to me. Now He is allowing me to share it with you.

I encourage everyone who reads or listens to these words to go directly to God Himself, Who is all The Truth, and ask Him what He wants you to know.

He will tell you.

> *You will hear*
> *your Teacher's Voice behind you.*
> *You will hear it*
> *whether you turn to the right or the left.*
> *It will say,*
> *"Here is the path I want you to take.*
> *So, walk on it."*
> *Isaiah 30:21*

INTRODUCTION

Do you remember when you were in your mother's womb? Most of us would say no, we don't remember being there. But we were there once.

So we know it is possible we were somewhere in a time before we remember. We were. We have always been alive and shall be forever.

I invite you back into the world of wonder from which you came. It was a time without time. It was a place with unlimited Joy. You were tucked safely into the very Heart of God Himself.

You would have perhaps chosen to stay there forever. But God had other plans for you. You were part of His Mission to a place called earth.

He sent you here from Heaven and He came with you.

The goal of The Mission is simple. Establish Heaven on earth.

Your Kingdom come,
Your Will be done,
on earth as it is in Heaven.
Matthew 6:10

Chapter One
YOUR BEGINNING

When did your life begin?

Many people would immediately think of their earth birthday. Some might think further back to the moment of their conception.

But, in fact, you were alive before you had an earth body.

David said,
"Your Eyes saw my <u>unformed</u> body."
Psalm 139:16

God said through the prophet, Jeremiah,
"<u>Before</u> I formed you in the womb,
I knew you."
Jeremiah 1:5

Paul said,
"He chose us in Him

<u>before the foundation of the world.</u>"
Ephesians 1:4

You have always been alive, tucked within God, as a part of Him.

You lived together in a time and place you have forgotten. Just as you have no memory of your life in your mother's womb, you have no recollection of that time and place...except now and then.

When you wonder if this human life is really all there is, a little Voice whispers, "You know there is so much more. Remember."

For a second, you think you do. Are you imagining it or was there really a world before this one?

Are you just hoping or do you feel assured there is a life after this one?

Why do we have these little mini awakenings?

Because God has created us with that time and place we call Eternity implanted within us.

Because God, The Creator of that awesomely large place, is also somehow tiny enough to be inside us.

The writer of Ecclesiastes understood part, but not all. He said,

> "He(God) has made everything
> beautiful in its time.
> <u>He has also set Eternity in the human heart</u>;
> yet no one can fathom what God has done
> from beginning to end."
> Ecclesiastes 3:11

We have tried to make Eternity fit in our human box of time. We cannot think outside that box.

But Jesus revealed Eternity is not about time. It is about recognizing who we are in God, with no beginning and no end.

> Jesus, talking to His Father God, said,
> "Now this is Eternal Life:
> that they know You,
> The Only True God,
> and Jesus Christ,
> Whom You have sent."
> John 17:3

Let's begin by going back to the time before time.

Chapter Two
BEFORE TIME

The Bible begins with "in the beginning."

In the beginning
God created the heavens and the earth.
Genesis 1:1

When John tried to describe the time before time in words we could understand, he had to write in earth terms. He could only think in terms of beginnings and endings.

So John said,
"In the beginning..."
John 1:1

But actually God had no "beginning" as we understand beginnings. God was everywhere before any beginnings.

He filled every corner of every world and every creature in what we call our past, present and future universes. He knew all and saw all He would speak into physical form at just the right moment.

He was already in all and would remain in all. But He would not reveal Himself in each part of His Creation until the precise moment He planned.

Imagine a huge jig saw puzzle spread out across time and space. Then imagine God holding all the pieces and putting them in place at just the right moment to connect with the next piece. And with each piece added, The Whole of His Creation becomes clearer.

You were already a part of God's Masterpiece. You were in Him and He was in you. But He would not reveal you in physical form to the world until much later.

Your part of God's Great Story would come after He created Time. And in that time, He promised He had a Good Plan for your future together with Him.

"For I know the plans I have for you,"
declares The Lord,
"plans to prosper you and not to harm you,

plans to give you hope
and a future."
Jeremiah 29:11

For we are God's Masterpiece.
He has created us anew in Christ Jesus,
so we can do the good things
He planned for us long ago.
Ephesians 2:10

Chapter Three
CREATION

How did God create? He created by calling forth from Himself something He wanted to reveal.

The "something" was already a part of Him. At a given time, He simply called for it to come into the physical realm and be seen.

How did He do it? Read the first chapter of Genesis. God spoke. He called for what He wanted to appear, and it was so. It happened!

We do a variation of that when we speak. When we say a word, we are attempting to bring it to life in the person to whom we are speaking.

When we say, "cat," we are thinking of the feline animal we already had stored in our memory. We believe by speaking that word, we can cause our listener to access their memory bank and share the thought of a cat.

However, we can not make a cat by speaking of it. God can. How can He do it?

His Words are different from ours. Our words are used primarily to communicate with each other. God's Words both communicate and create.

God's Words are actually more than a collection of letters. They are alive!

Paul said,

> "For _The Word of God_
> _is alive_ and active.
> Sharper than any double-edged sword,
> it penetrates even to dividing
> soul and spirit, joints and marrow;
> it judges the thoughts
> and attitudes of the heart."
> Hebrews 4:12

When God sends forth a Word into the universe, He goes with it and whatever or whoever He speaks becomes alive because He is in it giving it life.

You are one of God's Words!

Chapter Four
THE FULLNESS OF TIME

G od had a Plan for earth and all its inhabitants before He created the world. He had it all mapped out like a gigantic jig saw puzzle.

He designed the shape and size of each piece. He colored each one. He designed each piece to fit perfectly with the pieces around it.

Each of us is like one of those puzzle pieces.

Even though we might not realize it, we are each a part of God's Grand Design of the overall picture.

With a jig saw puzzle, some pieces will not fit until other pieces have been put in place.

So it is with the timing of our arrival on earth. We arrived here at exactly the time God planned, but not before our ancestors.

We carry within us traces of all who came before us.

They were created and lived exactly at the time God planned so that "in the fullness of time" we would be born.

God planned for us to be here at this very time in history. He orchestrated everything to make it so. We are indeed called by Him.

That is why the Bible often relates some things happening "in the fullness of time."

> *There is a time for everything*
> *and a season for every activity*
> *under the heavens.*
> *Ecclesiastes 3:1*

> *With all wisdom and understanding,*
> *He made known to us*
> *the mystery of His Will*
> *according to His Good Pleasure,*
> *which He purposed in Christ,*
> *to be put into effect*
> <u>*when the times reach their fulfillment*</u>—
> *to bring unity to all things in heaven*
> *and on earth under Christ.*
> *Ephesians 1:8-10*

All the days ordained for me
were written in Your Book
before one of them came to be.
Psalm 139:18

Chapter Five
GOD CALLED YOU!

So how did you come about? In the fullness of time, God spoke you into existence.

You might have visions of Him speaking and you instantly appearing. But that is not how Creation happens.

Creation is a process. There are many theories about how long it took for God to create the world as we know it.

But one thing we do know from observing the earth and everything on it. It takes time for anything or anyone to become what it is.

And in fact, everything and everyone is still being shaped and continually created by God. His Creation never stops.

We can begin to see how God put everything together like a huge jig saw puzzle across time and space.

But in order to increase our understanding, we have to understand His picture of the world is not a "one and done."

He is continually changing us and the world around us, fitting us together in new ways to fulfill His Mission.

Sometimes He takes pieces off the earth board and returns them to Himself.

Sometimes He changes our shape and moves us to a new part of the board. The puzzle picture changes. God remains the same.

But for now, let's go back to that time when God called you to become a part of His Earth picture.

Remember you were once a Word inside God waiting to be spoken. And when God spoke you into existence, you would come filled with Him inside you.

You can find your origin in John's description.

In the beginning was The Word,
and The Word was with God,

and The Word was God.
He was with God in the beginning.
John 1:1-2

You can put your name as one of God's Words.

So I can say,
"In the beginning, there was Carolyn.
I was with God.
I was a part, but not all of God.
All of me was God,
but I was not all of God."

I was with God in the beginning. So were you.

Then at just the time He planned, He called you to come into the physical world.

Chapter Six
PACKED FOR MISSION EARTH

Before bringing you to earth, God carefully considered the part you would play in His overall Mission.

He packed inside you your God given talents. Everyone received talents, but not all are alike. He gave each of us just what we need to carry out our part of His Plan.

Paul said,
"There are different kinds of gifts,
but The Same Spirit distributes them.
There are different kinds of service,
but The Same Lord.

There are different kinds of working,
but in all of them and in everyone
it is The Same God at work."
1 Corinthians 12:4-6

We are given those gifts for us to enjoy and to benefit other people. But more importantly, we are given those gifts so God can work through us in carrying out His Mission to earth. As Paul says, it is God at work.

Paul says,
"All these are the work
of one and The Same Spirit,
and He distributes them
to each one,
just as He determines."
1 Corinthians 12:11

Paul goes on to explain how we are each a part of God, Who revealed Himself as a human in The Body of Jesus.

We in ourselves are not all of God. But God is in each of us. We see more of God the more we allow Him to work through us and when we actively look to see Him in everyone He created.

So who are you? Paul answered that one too.

> *For we are God's Masterpiece.*
> *He has created us anew*
> *in Christ Jesus,*
> *so we can do the good things*
> *He planned for us long ago.*
> *Ephesians 2:10*

Chapter Seven
ANGELS

God Himself is both inside and outside us on our mission to earth.

God also has brought helpers for us. God created other beings called angels. They love God, praise Him and serve Him in helping us carry out our mission on earth.

Angels are able to go back and forth between heaven and earth.

Jacob saw
"a stairway resting on the earth,
with its top reaching to heaven,
and the angels of God
were ascending and descending on it."
Genesis 28:12

They bring messages from God. They guide and guard us.

They have other abilities we do not have.

They are not limited by time, place or distance. They seem to be able to appear in different physical forms, including human form.

They are sometimes seen by humans, but not recognized as angels.

Angels are a whole different type of created being from humans. While they may temporarily appear as humans, they are never really truly human. They are angels.

We do not become angels when we leave the earth. We were made in The Image of God from the beginning. When we shed our earth suit, we will be like Jesus. We will be higher than angels.

When Christ appears,
we shall be like Him,
for we shall see Him as He is.
1 John 3:2

But while we are on earth, we, like Jesus, are made to be a little lower than the angels. We cannot do all they do.

Even though that is true now, we also have The Promise that what was true for Jesus will also be true for us.

Paul said,
"You made them
a little lower than the angels;
you crowned them with glory and honor
and put everything under their feet.

In putting everything under them,
God left nothing
that is not subject to them.
Yet at present
we do not see everything
subject to them.

But we do see Jesus,
Who was made lower than the angels
for a little while,
now crowned with glory and honor!"
Hebrews 2:7-9

Chapter Eight
YOU WERE A PLANNED PREGNANCY!

How were you created? Were you a result of a planned pregnancy or not?

If you are reading this, you can be absolutely assured God planned for you to be born.

What happens outside a woman's body is not always holy. Real Love can be expressed in human ways outside a woman's body. However, what happens there is not always Love or a Holy Meeting.

It is not always planned or even desired. Decisions made outside the body fall within our free will.

But what happens on the inside is completely up to God. Once sperm is released, it will either find its way to the egg or it will not.

Sperm would never meet egg unless God desired it to be so. You may have been unplanned or even unwanted by humans.

But you were planned by God and very much wanted by Him.

We must never forget Jesus' conception was very unplanned by those who were integral in God's Creation and Revelation of Himself as Jesus.

What the angel told Mary is also true for you. Remember you are one of God's Words. And once He called for you, there was no stopping Him. He wanted you to be revealed on earth.

For No Word from God will ever fail!
Luke 1:37

Chapter Nine
AWESOMELY MADE

Y ou have always been spirit. You have been part of the Great Spirit of God. You will always be that spirit, whether in a human body or out of it.

Much as the astronauts have special suits to wear when they leave earth, you have an "earth suit" to wear while you are here.

That earth suit is your body. God has equipped it with everything you need to function in this environment. He will personally keep it functioning as long as He wants you to be on earth.

When your earth assignment is complete, God will shut down your earth suit and your spirit will return to The Wholeness of God, as you were before your earth trip.

The dust returns to the ground it came from,
and the spirit returns to God Who gave it.
Ecclesiastes 12:7

Each earth suit is different. There is no one who is exactly like anyone else on earth. But we have many things in common.

We have hearts, lungs, stomachs and a whole lot of other things that are alike. Because we look or act differently on the outside, we sometimes forget how alike we are.

David pondered how God made him and was absolutely awed.

David said,
"For You created my inmost being;
You knit me together
in my mother's womb.
I praise You because
I am fearfully and wonderfully made;
Your Works are wonderful,
I know that full well."
Psalm 139:13-14

So now we come to a question that many have asked. Does God create imperfect bodies? No, He does not.

He creates each body for their specific mission on earth. What we view as imperfect is absolutely perfect in The Eyes of The Creator. He created each body in His Time and for His Purpose.

When Jesus was asked why the man was born blind, He answered.

"This happened
so that The Works of God
might be displayed in him."
John 9:3

Some might think The Works of God were only displayed when Jesus changed earth blindness into earth seeing that day.

But, in fact, The Works of God had been on display for all of that man's life, for all who had the spiritual sight to see it.

We can say we do not understand God's Plan, but we should never judge God's Work as flawed.

God said we would not always understand.

"For My Thoughts are not your thoughts,
neither are your ways My Ways,"
declares The Lord.

"As the heavens
are higher than the earth,
so are My Ways
higher than your ways
and My Thoughts
than your thoughts."
Isaiah 55:8-9

We can rest easy that God has created every body for a purpose and He is working out His Perfect Plan.

Chapter Ten
HARDWIRED

God made us with many features "hardwired in." We cannot change them. We can try to rebel against His Design, believing we can do better.

But resistance is futile. God will prevail. Sadly we are often like toddlers kicking, screaming and demanding our own way when our Father God is leading us on the best way.

We cannot change the time of our arrival or departure from earth. We cannot rip out our heart and expect to live.

We cannot change our assignment on this mission.

We were given the external covering God wanted us to have.

We were given the talents He wanted us to have.

We cannot recreate ourselves into anyone other than who God created us to be.

We cannot make God come in and go out of us. He created us to be with Him permanently around us, inside us, and all through us. We can never do anything to separate ourselves from God.

God's Constant Presence is by His Design, not our choice.

> *You did not choose Me,*
> *but I chose you*
> *and appointed you*
> *so that you might go and bear fruit —*
> *fruit that will last.*
> *John 15:16*

So are we robots? Do we get to choose anything or is it all up to God?

When God completed the things that are "hard wired," He was not done. He then added a very interesting feature.

He gave each person something called "free will."

Chapter Eleven
ARE WE ROBOTS?

If God has pre-planned everything and is in charge of everything, are we just robots that can only do what He wants?

No! God created us with the very interesting feature called "free will." We can choose whether we will do what He wants or not.

But we need to understand there are consequences for bad choices. Is this God's punishment? No. It is a cause and effect.

We can put boundaries up to protect our children from running into the street. We can teach them not to go in the street unless they are holding our hand.

But if they refuse to obey and run into the street and get hit by a car, will it be us punishing them? No. It will, in part, be a result of their choice not to obey.

God gives us boundaries. But He does not take away our ability to choose. He told Adam and Eve what to avoid. He told them what would happen if they chose not to obey.

But He let them choose their path. When they chose to disobey, they suffered the natural consequences of their choice.

How do we know where the boundaries are? How do we know what God wants us to do and what He does not want us to do?

God gave us an internal GPS. Read on to find out more about your God Positioning System!

Chapter Twelve
GPS

God did not send us to earth alone with just a set of instructions to follow. He did not set up a system where if we make a mistake, he punishes us severely.

We do not have to use trial and error, constantly banging our heads against walls we did not know were there.

God does not send us anywhere He is not going. He is in us and we are in Him. We are together always.

God is our GPS. He is our God Present Savior. He is always present and always our protector and defender, truly our Savior.

He has already set the destination. He knows how long it will take us to get there. But He also knows there are different ways to get there.

We choose the path, but He sets the boundaries. When we stray too far off course, He will set off the alarm to encourage us to make a course correction.

We sometimes refer to that alarm as our conscience.

How do we hear God?

He will speak from multiple directions in multiple ways.

Sometimes He will speak through what we might think are our own thoughts.

Sometimes He will speak through the words or actions of someone else.

Sometimes He will speak through the natural world around us.

Paul said,
"Since the creation of the world
God's invisible qualities—
His Eternal Power and Divine Nature—
have been clearly seen,
being understood

from what has been made,
so that people are without excuse."
Romans 1:20

Before we go inside this awesome body God has created for us, let's look around at what He has created outside our bodies.

Chapter Thirteen
GOD IS EVERYWHERE!

Look up. Look down. Look around. See the sky, the clouds, trees, flowers, weeds, rocks, birds, insects, animals and more.

Everything in all creation was made by God. He is in it right now giving it the life He designed it to have.

One God and Father of all,
Who is over all
and through all
and in all.
Ephesians 4:6

All things were made through Him,
and without Him nothing was made
that was made.
1 John 1:3

What we think are inanimate objects are anything but. They are alive, filled with God testifying of His Presence.

The heavens declare The Glory of God;
the skies proclaim The Work of His Hands.
Psalm 19:1

The morning stars sang together
and
all the angels shouted for joy.
Job 38:7

You will go out in joy
and be led forth in peace;
the mountains and hills
will burst into song before you,
and all the trees of the field
will clap their hands.
Isaiah 55:12

Jesus said,
"I tell you,
if they keep silent,
the stones will cry out!"
Luke 19:40

Holy, holy, holy
is The Lord Almighty;
the whole earth is full of His Glory!
Isaiah 6:3

God reveals Himself in what we see and hear and feel. He sometimes reveals Himself in things so familiar to us we may miss Him. He calls to us to look again.

Sometimes God reveals Himself through nature in ways that do not line up with our usual perception. Burning bushes, donkeys that talk, whales that provide safe passage and others.

Jesus and other teachers referred to nature for their examples. They were saying, "Let's start with something you think you know. Then we will move up to amazing things you can't even imagine yet!"

God loves everything He has created. He calls stars by name. He created His precious humans from the dust of the earth and returns their body to it when the mission is over.

Jesus spoke of how much care God gave to the flowers.

"Consider how the wildflowers grow.
They do not labor or spin.
Yet I tell you,
not even Solomon in all his splendor
was dressed like one of these."
Luke 12:27

Speaking of the sparrows, Jesus said,
"Not one of them will fall
to the ground
outside your Father's Care."
Matthew 10:29

God loves all He has created. Part of our earth mission is to care for all around us. We are here to be farmers, planting and growing the seeds of Heaven!

Chapter Fourteen
GOD IN YOU

God took care of every detail in planning for our mission to earth.

He planned the time of our arrival and the time of our departure. He packed us with talents and abilities to use while we are here.

He chose our traveling companions.

He sent angels with us.

He created the most amazing transport vehicle and mobile home anyone could imagine. The human body has so many bells and whistles that even the smartest people on the planet have not discovered them all yet.

God did all this for us. But He was not done. The absolute peak of God's Plan was so unique many would not even grasp it.

What else did God place inside you?

He placed Himself! He filled every part of you.

Jesus said,
"On that day you will realize
that I am in My Father,
and you are in Me,
and I am in you."
John 14:20

Paul was surprised that some of his followers did not remember.

Paul said,
"Do you not know
that your bodies are temples
of The Holy Spirit, Who is in you,
Whom you have received from God?
You are not your own!"
1 Corinthians 6:19

Exactly how close is God? He revealed the answer to that question to a young shepherd boy named David.

Chapter Fifteen
How Close Is God?

David started thinking about God in him. At first he was awe struck at realizing he was a masterpiece of The Creator of The Universe.

But then he moved on to consider God's Presence. And he was stunned to realize God had been, was and always would be with him.

Even if he wanted to be separate for just a second, he could never be apart from God. Neither can you.

David penned his thoughts in Psalm 139. He wrote them talking to God. But what he said was only confirming what God had first said to him.

The following is what God says to you and me too. It is taken from Psalm 139.

I have searched you and I know you.

I know when you sit and when you rise; I perceive

your thoughts.

I discern your going out and your lying down; I am familiar with all your ways.

Before a word is on your tongue, I, The Lord, know it completely.

I hem you in behind and before, and I lay My Hand upon you.

Such knowledge is so wonderful for you!

You wonder where you can go from My Spirit? Where can you flee from My Presence?

If you go up to the heavens, I am there; if you make your bed in the depths, I am there.

If you rise on the wings of the dawn, if you settle on the far side of the sea, even there My Hand will guide you, My Right Hand will hold you fast.

If you say, "Surely the darkness will hide me and the light become night around me," even the darkness will not be dark to Me; the night will shine like the day, for darkness is as light to Me.

For I created your inmost being; I knit you together in your mother's womb.

You are awesomely and wonderfully made; My Works are wonderful, you must know that full well.

Your frame was not hidden from Me when I made you in the secret place, when I wove you together in the depths of the earth.

My Eyes saw your unformed body; all the days ordained for you were written in My Book before one of them came to be.

Whether you are asleep or awake, I am still with you!

Jesus said,
"Be sure of this.
I am with you always!"
Matthew 28:20

Chapter Sixteen
WHAT CAN SEPARATE US FROM GOD?

Absolutely nothing.

Who is God? John told us in one simple statement.

God is Love.
1 John 4:8

And Paul tells us some amazing things about The Power of God's Love.

Paul had a rough and rugged life. And yet, after all he had done and all that had been done to him, he came to an important conclusion.

His conclusion was identical to what David expressed through Psalm 139.

Absolutely nothing could ever separate Him from God, Who was, is and ever shall be pure Love!

Notice Paul said he was "convinced." He was saying he had enough life experiences to test it out. His thoughts were not something he was wondering about. It was something he had come to know beyond a shadow of a doubt.

God did not just send His Love. He was present everywhere in everyone as Love. And no power on heaven, earth or hell itself can ever separate anyone from God and His Love.

Read through Paul's list and absorb it.

> *For I am convinced that*
> *neither death nor life,*
> *neither angels nor demons,*
> *neither the present nor the future,*
> *nor any powers,*
> *neither height nor depth,*
> *nor anything else in all creation,*
> *will be able to separate us*
> *from The Love of God*
> *that is in Christ Jesus our Lord.*
> *Romans 8:38-39*

Death cannot separate you from God.

Nothing in Life can separate you from God.

No angel can stand between you and God.

No demon can separate you from God.

Your past is over. It no longer exists.

Whatever is happening in this present time cannot separate you from God.

Nothing in the future can separate you from God.

There is no power in the entire universe that can separate you from God.

There is nothing higher than God.

There is nothing deeper than God.

Absolutely nothing in all creation can separate you from God.

You were always together, are now and ever shall be. It is so by His Choice.

Why has He done this? He has work to do in this time and place and He is going to do it n the same way as He did it through Jesus.

God as Jesus said,
"You did not choose Me,
but I chose you
and appointed you
so that you might go and bear fruit—
fruit that will last ..."
John 15:16

Chapter Seventeen
GOD'S BODY

In the opening chapter of Genesis, God revealed He made us in His Image.

Take a moment and absorb that thought. When you look in the mirror, you are looking at God. The real you is an awesome reflection of Him.

God revealed as Jesus gave another confirming statement.

Jesus said,
"This is My Body,
Which is given for you."
Luke 22:19

Many times people think of the broken, mangled body of the crucified Jesus and believe that is what He gave.

But what He really gave us was the awesomely created body we now wear. It is from our body He continues to minister.

Jesus said,
"On that day
you will realize that
I am in My Father,
and you are in Me,
and I am in you."
John 14:20

This might be that day for you. You are indeed made in the Image of God because He is inside you!

Paul said,
"Do you not know
that your bodies are temples
of The Holy Spirit, Who is in you,
Whom you have received from God?
You are not your own!"
1 Corinthians 6:19

Your eyes, ears, mouth, hands, feet, every part of you is His. You cannot live apart from Him. He created you to be together with Him.

Remember nothing could stop God's bringing you into the world. He had plans for what He and you were going to do together.

God chose you.

> *You did not choose Me,*
> *but I chose you*
> *and appointed you*
> *so that you might go and bear fruit—*
> *fruit that will last.*
> *John 15:16*

God has created us to live together with Him in His Body on earth. But less we think more of ourselves than we should, there is something else to know about God's Body.

As awesome as it is, we in our body are only part of God's Body!

Chapter Eighteen
GOD'S WHOLE BODY

We are an important part of God's Body, but we are only a tiny fraction of it.

We are each like a drop of water compared to the ocean. Each of us is full of God, but we are individually not all of God.

We should never underestimate anyone by saying God is not in them. He is in everyone, even if they have not discovered Him yet.

By the same token, we should not overestimate our status or anyone else's. No one is on the same level as God. No one will ever be higher than God.

We cannot even think like God.

He told us,
*"My Thoughts are not your thoughts,
neither are your ways My Ways,"*
declares The Lord.

"As the heavens are higher than the earth,
so are My Ways higher than your ways
and My Thoughts than your thoughts."
Isaiah 55:8-9

God revealed Himself as Jesus, also called The Christ. Paul described God's Body.

Now you are The Body of Christ,
and each one of you
is a part of it.
1 Corinthians 12:27

In order to even begin to know God, we have to look for Him in each other. It takes all of us and all of God's Creations together from all times and places put together in just the right way to know God.

At what we call The Last Supper, Jesus took bread and broke it into pieces. He then gave a piece to each of His Disciples.

He told them the bread represented His Body, which He was giving to them.

He told them to remember Him.

This was more than just a simple wish for them to think about Him after His Death.

He was telling them He was giving a part of Himself to each of them to take into their own bodies. He had already identified Himself as The Bread of Life.

I am The Bread of Life.
John 6:35

He was telling them He was in each of their bodies and would continue to minister on earth through each of them.

But the real Power of His Body would only be felt when together they remembered Him.

This was more than a simple request for them to think of Him after He died. This simple instruction was the key to establishing Heaven on earth.

To remember Jesus is for each of us to join with the other and re-member His Body... put it back together in His Power.

Re-membering Jesus, Who is the physical manifestation of God, is to be willing to give all of ourselves back to God and to each other.

In The Garden, Jesus prayed, not only for those in that time, but also for us in our time and those in all times.

What did He pray?

"My prayer is not for them alone.
I pray also for those who will believe in Me
through their message,
that all of them may be one, Father,
just as You are in Me and I am in you.

May they also be in Us
so that the world may believe
that You have sent Me.

I have given them The Glory that You gave Me,
that they may be one as We are One —
I in them and You in Me —
so that they may be brought to complete unity.

Then the world will know
that You sent Me
and have loved them even as You have loved Me."
John 17:20-23

Chapter Nineteen
NAMED FOR THE MISSION

Now that God had prepared you for Mission Earth, He had one more important thing to do.

He named you. Your name is tied to your part of The Mission.

God named you by telling your parents what to call you. They may not have even been aware the idea for your name came from God.

But it did. Names are important to God. God calls the stars by name. He had Adam name the animals.

He told Zachariah what to call John.

He told Joseph what to name Jesus.

He told those responsible for you what to name you.

My parents lived in a time when it was common to name babies for relatives. However, both my parents felt I was to be named Carolyn.

No one else in the family was named Carolyn, but both my parents felt that was who I was born to be. They did not know the name had a meaning beyond identifying who I was.

But God knew.

Carolyn means "Song of Joy." I am absolutely thrilled to think of God singing over His new creation of me and speaking His Words,
"She shall be called Carolyn.
She is My Song of Joy!"

> *The Lord your God in your midst,*
> *The Mighty One, will save;*
> *He will rejoice over you with gladness,*
> *He will quiet you with His Love,*
> *He will rejoice over you with singing.*
> *Zephaniah 3:17*

God further blessed me by giving me the family name of Priester. He made me a Priest from the beginning.

To Him Who loves us
and has freed us from our sins
by His Blood,
and has made us to be
a kingdom and priests
to serve His God and Father—
to Him be Glory and power
for ever and ever! Amen.
Revelation 1:5-6

I do not always live up to my mission, but my name is a perpetual reminder of why God has brought me to earth.

I am here to be part of His Priesthood as a Song of Joy.

Research the meaning of your name. What has God called you to be? Who are you?

I have called you by name.
You are Mine!
Isaiah 43:1

Chapter Twenty
GOD'S NAME AND YOU

God gave you your name. But more than that, He gave you His Name.

Names are so important to God that He even named Himself.

God told Moses His Name is "I AM."

That sounds like a really strange name, but embedded in it is a Gift that will determine our destiny.

Remember God did not send us to earth alone. He came with us. We were together before time began, we are together now and so shall we ever be.

God gives us many resources to use while we are on planet earth. One of these is the right to use His Name.

In a marriage, sometimes the wife puts her husband's name after hers as a sign of their united relationship.

When I married Jay Jones, I began using his name after mine. I became Carolyn Priester Jones.

In a relationship with God, we should always put His Name first.

That is God's first instruction for using His Name. Nothing comes before Him.

But there is more. We must be very careful what we attach to God's Name. We are identifying who we are in Him.

He will not take kindly to anyone misusing His Name.

> **God said,**
> *"You shall not misuse*
> *The Name of The Lord your God,*
> *for The Lord will not hold anyone guiltless*
> *who misuses His Name."*
> *Exodus 20:7*

It is a given that pronouncing judgement in God's Name is not ok. So telling Him to damn anyone is out.

But there are other ways we can misuse God's Name.

We misuse God's Name when we put anything after it that does not line up with Who He is or who He says we are in Him.

When we say, "I am a sinner," God will not agree. He wants us to repent and not tarnish His Name by continuing to say we are sinners. He wants us to be able to say "I AM redeemed."

> He reminds us,
> *"I have redeemed you.*
> *I have called you by name.*
> *You are Mine."*
> *Isaiah 43:1*

When we say, "I am depressed" or "I am angry" or "I am not going to forgive," God will not agree.

Through The Power of His Name, God has given us a way to open doors on earth to let Heaven in.

Jesus used that Power. How did He do it?

Jesus said,
"I did not speak on My Own,
but The Father Who sent Me
commanded Me
to say all that I have spoken.

I know that His Command
leads to eternal life.
So whatever I say
is just what The Father
has told Me to say."
John 12:49-50

So be careful what you say. You, like Jesus, are a Messenger of God. You in yourself are limited, but remember The Power of The One inside you.

He has All Authority in Heaven and on earth.

And in The Power of His Name, He says,
"I AM with you always!"
Matthew 28:20

Chapter Twenty-One
ONE GOD

God is The Creator and Sustainer of all there is.

One God and Father of all,
Who is over all
and through all
and in all.
Ephesians 4:6

Are there different versions of God?

No.

God is so big we may see Him differently from different angles. But we cannot separate parts of Him from His Whole Self.

Even describing God as a Trinity is only our attempt to understand Him by compartmentalizing Him. It is not wrong, as long as we understand He will never be separate from any part of Himself.

God will reveal Himself in different ways, but He is One all the time. And He never acts against Himself.

God said through the prophet, Isaiah,

> *"I am The Lord,*
> *and there is no other,*
> *apart from Me there is no other."*
> *Isaiah 45:5*

When Jesus was asked which commandment was greatest of all, He answered,

> *"The most important is*
> *The Lord our God is One."*
> *Mark 12:29*

It was as if He was saying, "Understand this one thing and everything else will begin to make sense."

Who is God?

In Exodus 34:6-7,
God describes Himself as
"The Lord, The Lord,
The Compassionate and Gracious God,
slow to anger,
abounding in Love
and Faithfulness."

Because of God's Abounding Love, He did something spectacular to show His precious humans how He wanted them to live on earth.

He revealed Himself as both a Father and a Son. He called His Son, Jesus.

Chapter Twenty-Two
GOD BECOMES HUMAN!

After God prepared you to come to earth, He had one more important instruction for you.

"Be perfect,
therefore,
as your Heavenly Father is perfect."
Matthew 5:48

That sounds like an overwhelming expectation. Our first thought might be, "I can't do that. I am only human."

But we are more than human. Never forget that.

Jesus said,
"On that day you will realize
that I am in My Father,
and you are in Me,
and I am in you."
John 14:20

When you wonder how this is going to work, have no worries. God has a living human demonstration for you.

God packaged Himself as a human to show us how to live a perfect Life as a human.

> *The Word became flesh*
> *and made His dwelling*
> *among us.*
> *John 1:14*

He did this, not to sacrifice a human to please Him, but to save humans from falling into a hell on earth.

God did not want to just give us a pass after we sinned. He wanted to save us from sinning.

> The angel who foretold Jesus' birth
> told Joseph,
> *"You are to give Him The Name Jesus,*
> *because*
> *He will save His people from their sins."*
> *Matthew 1:21*

God revealed Himself as both a Father and a Son, so He could show us how to relate to Him.

In revealing Himself as Jesus, God essentially said, "Watch this. I am your Father.   You are my child. Let Me show you how this works."

Chapter Twenty-Three
FATHER AND SON

Why did God reveal Himself as what appeared to be two separate beings?

Jesus was God's Demonstration Project. So, what was God showing us in appearing both as a Father and a Son?

Relationship.

God wanted to show humans how to relate to Him. Jesus was the picture of what God created each of His Humans to be

Paul said,
"Put on your new nature,
and be renewed
as you learn to know your Creator
and become like Him.

Jesus is our pattern,
our example.
He is The One we are to follow,
to imitate."
Colossians 3:10

However, God wanted much more than humans imitating a human who was in human form for a limited time in a limited place.

God wanted His Precious Creations to recognize He was in their bodies the same as He was in Jesus' Body.

They would not have to imitate. They would simply have to recognize The Power inside them and surrender to it.

If they were forgetting what they were on earth to do, they could always remember Jesus and be reminded they had the same Power available to them as Jesus did.

We also can look at Jesus and be reminded God wants to do everything through us He did through Jesus.

Jesus said,
"Very truly I tell you,
whoever believes in Me
will do the works I have been doing,
and they will do
even greater things than these!"
John 14:12

But first we humans need to understand how God operates from the inside of a human body.

This begins with understanding it was God Himself inside the body of a man named Jesus.

The second we try to make Jesus separate from God is the moment the rest of the salvation story will veer off into misunderstanding.

Let's look at how what is One can appear to be more than One.

Chapter Twenty-Four
ONE GOD, MANY NAMES

While we may have difficulty seeing God and Jesus as One at the same time, we, in fact, can see "oneness" in ourselves.

I am a daughter, a wife, a mother, a grandmother and much more.

If my parents, my husband, my daughter and my grandson were with me in the same room, and we asked each who I was, we would get a different answer.

My parents would say I am Carolyn, their daughter. My husband would say I am Carolyn, his wife. My daughter would say I am Mom. My grandson would say I am Grandma.

Do I stop being Mom to be Grandma? No. In fact, I can be the daughter, wife, mother and grandmother all at the same time.

Who I am depends on the relationship, not the physical presence of a person.

God wanted us to understand He was literally everywhere. But we would relate to Him in different ways throughout our assignment on planet earth. And we would call Him by different names.

Sometimes we would see Him as a Father or Mother. Sometimes a baby or child as Jesus began life. Sometimes we would see Him as a friend, a traveling companion, a teacher, a healer, a protector, a counselor and more.

God revealed to the prophet, Isaiah, how He would be called by many different names.

> In foretelling Jesus' birth, Isaiah said,
> *"Behold—*
> *the virgin will have a child in the womb,*
> *and she will give-birth to a Son.*
> *And they will call His name Immanuel."*
> Isaiah 7:14

Matthew repeated this prophecy, adding the important explanation that Immanuel meant "God with us."

Behold,
the virgin shall conceive
and bear a Son,
and they shall call His Name Immanuel,
which means, God with us.
Matthew 1:23

Isaiah also foretold other Names of God revealed as Jesus. It is important to note they were not separate. They were One but seen different ways at different times.

"For a Child is born to us,
a Son is given to us.
The government will rest on His shoulders.
And He will be called:
Wonderful Counselor,
Mighty God,
Everlasting Father,
Prince of Peace."
Isaiah 9:6

And then the angel told Joseph what to call this Son.

She will give birth to a Son,
and you are to give Him
The Name Jesus,
because
He will save His people from their sins.
Matthew 1:21

And thus many call Jesus, The Savior.

But how exactly would God through Jesus save His People?

God had two more important Names. God revealed Himself as both a Father and a Son.

The angel told Mary that the child to be born to her would be called The Son of God.

The Holy One to be born
will be called
The Son of God!
Luke 1:35

Chapter Twenty-Five
FATHERS

Why did God reveal Himself as both a Father and a Son? He wanted us to understand how to relate to Him as who we truly are.

> **John said,**
> *See what great love*
> *The Father has lavished on us,*
> *that we should be called*
> *children of God!*
> *And that is what we are!*
> *1 John 3:1*

We can delight in being the children of a Loving Father. However, many have trouble seeing God as a loving Father.

Some have not had a loving Father on earth.

Some have had fathers who left them confused about what love is, punishing them severely and then telling them it was done for love.

Some have had fathers who used them and called their sexual abuse love.

Some had fathers who never approved of them. Every moment together was a performance test they failed.

Criticism, Accusations, Judgement and Punishment were a part of being the children of some earthly fathers.

Some had fathers who abandoned them.

Some had fathers who disowned them.

And some had Christian fathers who simply did not understand their own relationship as a child of God and passed on what they thought was Truth but was not.

So now we come to pivotal questions.

Is God really our Father?

Can we trust God our Father?

Can we ever really please Him?

Is He going to punish us severely every time we mess up?

Will He abandon us?

Is God a Good Father?

Chapter Twenty-Six
YOUR FATHER GOD

Is God a Good Father?

Yes, He is. Everything He demonstrated through His Relationship with Jesus is true about His Relationship with you.

God and Jesus were together before the beginning of time. So were you.

God planned for Jesus long before He was born to earth. He also planned you.

Jesus' conception happened inside the body of a human mother by an Act of God. So did your conception. Even if your birth was unplanned or unwanted by humans, sperm would never have met egg except through God.

God decided what Jesus would be called. God also named you.

God celebrated Jesus' birth. He was delighted to

welcome Him. He also celebrated your arrival on earth.

God was happy to publicly claim His Relationship with Jesus and tell everyone He loved Him. He is happy to do the same for you.

God allowed Jesus to be tempted by satan, but He never left Him. He reminded Him not to respond to satan's attempt to throw Him off course. He reminded Him of The Power of God's Word. He will do the same for you.

God was with Jesus all the time. He talked with Him and guided Him in everything He did.

God did not criticize or condemn Jesus for questioning His Plan. But He did not change The Plan. He loved Jesus and stayed with Him through every hard moment. He will do the same for you.

When His Mission was complete, God welcomed Him Home with Joy. He will do the same for you.

God is the best Father you could ever have. And, like Jesus, you are made in the Image of your Father.

The Father's goal is for you to be able to say to the world what Jesus said.

> *"If you have seen Me,*
> *you have seen The Father!"*
> *John 14:9*

And God is happy to say about you what He said of Jesus.

> *You are my child,*
> *whom I love;*
> *with you, I am well pleased.*
> *Matthew 3:17*

Chapter Twenty-Seven
DOES GOD LOVE ME?

Yes, God loves you! Remember He has been planning for you since the beginning of the world.

When He looks at you, He sees you as He created you to be. He sees His Child, made in His Image.

God created humans
in His Own Image,
in The Image of God
He created them.
Genesis 1:27

See what great love
The Father has lavished on us,
that we should be called
children of God!
And that is what we are!
1 John 3:1

God sees you as Paul recorded.

For we are God's Masterpiece,
created in Christ Jesus to do good works,
which God prepared in advance for us to do.
Ephesians 2:10

God said of Jesus,
"This is My Son,
Whom I love;
with Him I am well pleased."
Matthew 3:17

He says the same thing about you. You are His Child, Who He loves. He is well pleased with you.

You might think you do not deserve such an affirmation. You might think you are not even close to being Jesus. You might think you have not done enough things right to earn God's Love.

You would be right.

You cannot ever earn God's Love. He loves you not because of what you have done or not done. He loves you simply because you are His Creation, His Masterpiece.

In fact, He is so delighted with you that He even sings over you.

The Lord your God in your midst,
The Mighty One, will save;
He will rejoice over you with gladness,
He will quiet you with His love,
He will rejoice over you with singing.
Zephaniah 3:17

You never have to compare yourself to anyone else. God does not play favorites with His Children. He loves each of us completely for the unique person He created us to be. There is no one else in the entire world who is exactly like you.

God has always loved you, does now and will always. He will be constantly drawing you close.

I have loved you
with an Everlasting Love;
I have drawn you
with Unfailing Kindness.
Jeremiah 31:3

When He said "everlasting," He meant it. Nothing can ever separate you from God's Love.

Go back and re-read chapter 16 in this book!

Chapter Twenty-Eight
GOD'S CHILD

Do you want to be God's Child?

Many would immediately say, "Yes! Absolutely!"

But do you ever have any concerns about what God might ask you to do?

Do you ever listen to Easter stories and wonder why God gave His Son a really dirty job to do and then sat it out and looked the other way?

A prominent atheist actually said outright what many Christians may have secretly pondered.

The atheist said, "I could never trust a God Who would treat His Son like He did."

The old, old story has been told in a way that would give some credence to the atheist's conclusions.

Now let's be clear. The way he heard it and undoubtedly, the way we may have heard it, is not true.

The way the atheist heard it, God was angry with the people He had created. He wanted to beat them, torture them, desert them and finally kill them.

But God had a soft spot for His humans. So He sent His one and only Son to earth while He sat way off in Heaven. His Son would save some of the people, but the others would just be condemned to Hell.

God decided to issue a one-time pardon through sacrificing His Son like the people had sacrificed their animals.

His Son would be tortured and suffer an agonizing and public death. God wanted Him to be the example of what He wanted to do to the people, so they would turn from their evil ways out of fear of punishment.

God expected their unwavering allegiance for the rest of their lives and He wanted them to be sure to pass on the story so future generations would know to fear Him.

He also assured the cross, the instrument of torture, would become a centerpiece of worship and constant reminder of what could have happened to them if The Son had not taken their place.

Oh yes, by the way, the Son did make a reappearance after being killed, but He never stuck around. He went back to His Father. The people on earth hope He will be back one day.

That story is full of misconceptions. So, let's look at The Truth.

Chapter Twenty-Nine
WHO IS JESUS?

R eview Chapter Twenty-One.

There is One God.

He is in all and through all.

He is everywhere at once in all times and places.

He reveals parts of Himself at different times and in different ways.

He can reveal Himself in different ways at the same time.

God revealed Himself as a human named Jesus. Jesus is God in human form.

God also revealed Himself as Jesus' Father. He did this to teach us how to relate to Him in Love, not fear.

God is Love. He never does anything apart from Love.

When God appeared in human form as Jesus, He did not stop being God everywhere else. He fills all time and space, both inside and outside a human body.

But as Jesus, He said plainly He was One God.

Jesus said,
"I and The Father are One."
John 10:30

Jesus said,
"Believe Me when I say
that I am in The Father and
The Father is in Me."
John 14:11

Jesus said,
"Anyone who has seen Me
has seen The Father."
John 14:9

There are even more subtle cues that anyone who had seen Jesus had indeed seen God The Father. They are God winks!

**Jesus said,
"I am The True Vine,
and My Father is The Gardener."
John 15:1**

John 20:15 records Mary's conversation with Jesus after His Resurrection. She did not recognize Him. She thought He was the gardener. He was. Remember Jesus said, The Father is The Gardener!

The real story, is God Himself is Jesus. God loved us so much He was willing to compress Himself into a tiny human body and live a human life to teach us about Him.

He was willing to suffer everything satan could throw at Him. He did it because He loved His Precious humans.

God was never separate from Jesus because He was in Jesus and Jesus was in Him.

God never acts against HImself.

God's Revelation of Himself as Jesus never contradicted anything He had revealed of Himself in other ways.

Jesus was the only begotten Son of God, meaning He was conceived in a non-traditional way. But He was not the only child of God.

All who were created by God are His Children. That is why Jesus began what we call The Lord's Prayer by saying, "Our Father."

You are in God and He is in you.

In fact, you were created to be like Jesus! And that is to be in The Center of God's Love and Care.

Let's look at another part of the Easter Story that may have been misinterpreted over the years.

Chapter Thirty
WAS JESUS A SACRIFICE?

Was sacrificing Jesus a way to placate an angry God?

No!

God made it very clear what He thought about sacrifices.

Through the prophet Hosea, God said,
"For I desire mercy,
<u>*not sacrifice,*</u>
and acknowledgment of God
rather than burnt offerings"
Hosea 6:6

Jesus repeated God's Words when He said,
"Go and learn what this means:
'I desire mercy,
<u>*not sacrifice."*</u>
Matthew 9:13

In a stunning proclamation
that underscores God's intents,
Jesus said,
"If you had known what this means,
'I desire mercy,
<u>*not sacrifice,'*</u>
you would not have condemned
the guiltless."
Matthew 12:7

So it cannot be true that God would present Jesus as a sacrifice to please Him. God did not want sacrifice. He wanted mercy. He wanted acknowledgement of Him.

By placing Himself on the most heinous instrument of torture for that day, God was able to show the full extent of His Mercy.

He looked out on the world and demonstrated the ultimate Mercy. As Jesus, He interceded for us.

He said,
"Father, forgive them.
They do not know
what they are doing."
Luke 23:34

And God The Father said it was done.
"It is finished."
John 19:30

So who put Jesus on the cross? God went there Himself. He chose the path. He walked the path. He allowed satan and his demons to take their best shot.

Why? He wanted to expose evil. Bring it out into full view. Show the worst of the worst so He could show the best of the best.

And God did it all for each one of us. He is a very Good Father.

Chapter Thirty-One
WHY THE CROSS?

The cross was the most extreme public demonstration of evil in that day. It rolled humiliation, shame, torture, pain and more all into one show.

After the torture, there was never any doubt its victims were dead.

There is no way God would have wanted the suffering of the cross for any of His precious humans.

But He knew His going to the cross would do several things.

It would graphically expose evil.

It would prove beyond a shadow of a doubt Jesus was dead.

God would prove beyond a shadow of a doubt that death could not defeat Him.

God would defeat death and take away the dread of it.

> **Paul said,**
> *"Since we, God's children,*
> *are human beings—*
> *made of flesh and blood—*
> *He became flesh and blood too*
> *by being born in human form;*
>
> *for only as a human being*
> *could He die*
> *and in dying break the power of the devil*
> *who had the power of death.*
>
> *Only in that way could He deliver*
> *those who through fear of death*
> *have been living all their lives*
> *as slaves to constant dread."*
> *Hebrews 12:13-15*

God would demonstrate to His humans what He had taught them earlier.

"I have told you these things,
so that in Me,
you may have peace.
In this world you will have trouble.
But take heart!
I have overcome the world."
John 16:33

On the cross, God brought home another resounding Truth.

The wages of sin is death,
but The Gift of God is Eternal Life
in Christ Jesus our Lord.
Romans 6:23

Sin will always demand to pay us what we earned. God stands ready to gift us with what we can never earn.

But He will not force us. We have a choice.

On the cross, God graphically illustrated exactly what that choice was.

I call on Heaven and earth
as witnesses today that
I have offered you
Life or death,
Blessings or curses.
Choose Life
so that you and your descendants
will live.
Deuteronomy 30:19

The cross exposed all the worst of evil. It put it on public display.

But the cross also showed the best of Heaven and earth. Love, Mercy and Grace.

And for those who look into The Face of Jesus, they see The Face of God.

Anyone who has seen Me
has seen The Father!
John 14:9

Chapter Thirty-Two
THE MISSION

When God exited The Body of Jesus, He was not done. He simply retired The Body of Jesus and continued His Work through every body He had created.

Jesus' Words echo what He The Father whispered in your ear from the moment He created you.

"This is My Body,
given for you."
Luke 22:19

Paul repeated it.
"Your body is The Temple of The Holy Spirit,
Who is in you,
Whom you have received from God.
You are not your own."
1 Corinthians 6:19

Remember God's Plan from before the beginning was to be with every person He created. And so

He was, is and shall be.

In Jesus, God gave the virtual demonstration of how humans could live the life He wanted them to have.

> *"I have come that*
> *they may have Life,*
> *and have it to the full!"*
> *John 10:10*

> *"I am The Way*
> *and The Truth*
> *and The Life."*
> *John 14:6*

As Jesus, God taught them. He lived the human life right in front of them. He had all the experiences humans had.

He demonstrated how to stay connected to Him.

He demonstrated Love, Mercy and Grace.

He forgave what seemed unforgivable.

He healed what seemed incurable.

He chose those others rejected.

Jesus said we would do even greater things than He did. How is that possible?

Because God never was limited to one body. He is in every body He has created. His Presence is by His Design, not by our choice.

You did not choose Me,
but I chose you
and appointed you
so that you might go
and bear fruit—
fruit that will last.
John 15:16

God is The Power that gave us Life before He gave us an earth body and He will continue to give us Life after our earth body has transitioned back to a Heavenly body.

God is inside each of us, just as He was inside The Body of Jesus.

He said the day would come when you would know. Perhaps you knew before today. Or maybe today is your day.

Jesus said,
"On that day you will realize
that I am in My Father,
and you are in Me,
and I am in you."
John 14:20

God, your Loving Father, Who planned you before time and created you when it was time, now is calling you at this time to complete The Mission for which He has brought you to earth.

You have been sent from Heaven with one mission. Jesus clearly stated it. Establish The Kingdom of Heaven on earth.

Behold!
The Kingdom of God
is within you!
Luke 17:21

Your Kingdom come on earth,
as it is in Heaven.
Matthew 6:10

"Therefore," Jesus said,
"Go and make disciples
of all the nations,
baptizing them in
The Name of
The Father and The Son
and The Holy Spirit.

Teach these new disciples
to obey all the commands
I have given you.

And be sure of this:
I am with you always!"
Matthew 28:19-20

A Few Imparting Words

There is much to be done to fulfill The Mission to which we have been called. The time for our earth assignment has already been set by God.

He is The One Who created us and called us into physical form in the fullness of time.

When our part of His Great Mission is complete, He will escort us Home to once more be in that timeless, ageless world freed of the restrictions of earth.

If we have spent our time here wisely, we will be able to say what Jesus said.

"I have brought You Glory on earth
by finishing the work
You gave me to do.

And now, Father,
glorify me in Your Presence
with The Glory I had with You
before the world began."
John 17:4-5

And we will hope to hear God say,
"Well done,
good and faithful servant.
Enter into The Joy of your Lord!"
Matthew 25:23

PARTING BLESSING

*Now, there are many other things
that Jesus did.
If they were all written down
one by one,
I suppose that the whole world
could not hold the books
that would be written.
John 21:25*

I would like to add to those books by potentially making this the first book in a series.

If The Lord so allows, with His Direction, I would be honored to write the next book about fulfilling our mission by living with God in us.

We will have to wait and see what He has planned.

In the meantime, I will pray for you, the readers and listeners of this book. And I will be thankful for your prayers as we continue the journey together.

If you would like to contact me, you can do so either by email to

carolynpriesterjones@gmail.com

Or

through my blog at

carolynpriesterjones.org

Many blessings to you!

Carolyn Priester Jones